# PRAISE FOR *CAN I KICK IT?*

"*Can I Kick It?* is an essential text, not just for its imagery, or its lyric, or its commitment to history. But, most importantly, for the way Idris Goodwin, once again, builds worlds. Yes, of course the wordplay is as on point as ever—incisive and playful and still not to be played with. But I can also feel the walls of the house party. I can feel myself in the seats of old movie theaters. And that is the true gift of this book. It creates spaces worth longing for, even if you don't remember the time when you longed for them."

—**Hanif Abdurraqib**, author of *Go Ahead in the Rain: Notes to A Tribe Called Quest*

"Idris Goodwin is the Chicago cousin of Motown, hip-hop, and b-ball. His literary scriptures are rooted in the BreakBeat Poets' pedagogical theory and soar in the spirit of the boom bap, the one-two, and the crossover. Goodwin's contemporary emboldened eulogies cipher the forgotten founders of hood politics, the crooners in the corner of the juke joint with a precision so clean, his readers sway between the syntax as both witness and worship. These poems name our rising stars ('Of the Lord') and our unsung deities ('An Ode to Lotion'). This text is beyond the truth. This text is a book of questions that will center and survive the political body surviving both PSSD & PTSD, one stanza at a time."

—**Mahogany L. Browne**, author of *Black Girl Magic, Smudge,* and *Redbone*

"*Can I Kick It?* is an anthem for the generation Idris Goodwin dubs 'A Tribe Called Tomorrow.' In this new collection, he charts the topographies of his personal, political, artistic, and cultural landscapes, while weaving together ancestral echoes, 80s-pop-culture references, Missy Elliot and Isiah Thomas. All the while, we're immersed in a soundtrack laced with the rhythms of gospel, Motown, house, and hip-hop. It is a nostalgia-tinged nod to the past, a chronicling of our chaotic present, and a questioning of what is yet to come. In 'Harriet Tubman to Kanye West' Tubman advises Yeezy to 'always rewind/ listen to the voices on the track/ before saying a word.' With *Can I Kick It?*, Goodwin not only puts this advice to good use but also embodies it with every line and bar."

—**Mayda A. Del Valle**, author of *A South Side Girl's Guide to Love & Sex*

"Idris Goodwin's poems are funny and searing at the same time. Goodwin is a poet of lyric precision and masterful invention. Ranging from odes to how-to guides to persona poems in the voices of DJ Khaled, Harriet Tubman, and more, Goodwin's *Can I Kick It?* reads the way my favorite albums play. Read it straight through. No skips necessary."

—**José Olivarez**, author of *Citizen Illegal*

"Idris Goodwin is at his best when he that rat-a-tat-tat, like the rhythms right before that crossover, or when 9th Wonder be channeling that God Theadore or his Godfather Preemo, or just when that gun-play reminds us that this life is real, all of that, all of that, so take this as word, that *Can I Kick It?* is Goodwin at his best."

—**Dr. Mark Anthony Neal**, James B. Duke Professor of African & African American Studies at Duke University

"In *Can I Kick It?*, Idris Goodwin gifts readers with sharp responses to today's injustices with humor, heart, and wit. Whether tackling *Charlie and the Chocolate Factory*, ashy skin, Ferris Bueller, *Game of Thrones*, legendary dunks, or Kanye, Goodwin's poems are how we exercise our freedom to claim a space with 'words of daily reclaiming.' This book holds a discography of a breakbeat upbringing, odes that uplift, and steady reminders that 'everything belongs to the beat.'"

—**Juan J. Morales**, author of *The Handyman's Guide to End Times*

# CAN I KICK IT?

# The BreakBeat Poets Series

## ABOUT THE BREAKBEAT POETS SERIES

The BreakBeat Poets series, curated by Kevin Coval and Nate Marshall, is committed to work that brings the aesthetic of hip-hop practice to the page. These books are a cipher for the fresh, with an eye always to the next. We strive to center and showcase some of the most exciting voices in literature, art, and culture.

## BREAKBEAT POETS SERIES TITLES INCLUDE:

# IDRIS GOODWIN

Haymarket Books
Chicago, Illinois

Published in 2019 by
Haymarket Books
P.O. Box 180165
Chicago, IL 60618
www.haymarketbooks.org

ISBN: 978-1-64259-027-2

Distributed to the trade in the US through Consortium Book Sales and Distri-
bution (www.cbsd.com) and internationally through Ingram Publisher Services
International (www.ingramcontent.com).

This book was published with the generous support of Lannan Foundation and
Wallace Action Fund.

Cover design by John Yates. Photo credit Andrew Cenci. Custom handstyle by
KEO XMEN / Blake Lethem.
Book design by Jamie Kerry.

Printed in Canada by union labor.

10 9 8 7 6 5 4 3 2 1

# CONTENTS

# Back to the Afro-Future, 1965

And I've arrived to roam a pre-riot
pre-crack Detroit where the blocks
are filled with fathers

And because my teenage dad
don't need lessons on game
and no brothers named Biff

No meddling necessary

My time free so I spin wild
with Doc Brown named
because of his likeness to Julius Erving

Plate in his head thanks to shrapnel
a parting gift from the service
where he was in communications

We tinker with some stereo equipment
some old record players, we raid
the 45s and at the Get Down Under the Sea dance
I blend the Temptations into the Tops

And Mary Wells into the Supremes
but that James Brown *I Feel Good*
smuggled in the passenger of the DeLorean
get 'em grooving and I get that feeling too

I start cutting it up
crab, transform
scratch, blend

The DJ who hurt his head rushes to long distance call his Caribbean cousin
"Yo Clive, you know that new sound you been looking for?"
and the whole thing spin-full

*1*

I am Grandmaster Flash, Grandmaster DST, Jam Master Jay, Cut Creator,
Qbert cutting up the same James Brown records they will cut
for the next fifty years until the end of time

I look up at the crowd for the first time
They give that look only
aggravated Black folk can

This is the era of harmony, Hendrix has yet to shred metal
They don't know 'bout Black noise over the measure
only black noise in the dark. Hell they not even wearing Afros yet

"Guess ya'll not ready" I say "but ya kids gonna love it"

# We Wear the Metal Face

*He hold his heart when he telling rhyme.*

—MF Doom

Surprised by the smile
But anger is dialed
To a simmer but the lid easy to lift
Buttons easy to push, easy to flip

Switch

face metal but liquid
solid but fluid
improvise off a blueprint
mood in the music

villain who shape
shift, a creature who ape
shit, believe in the great
gifts, retreat in a space
ship

# World of Rap

*When you say rap, there's varieties*
*rap that's kinda pop.*
*SoundCloud rap.*
*Then there's the real rap.*
*There's rap that's a mix between real real rap,*
*commercial rap, and underground rap.*

—Bhad Bhabie

There's all type of rap

Rap prayers
Rap gibberish
Rap Morse code
Rap lullabies
sleepy-time-rhymes
Rap dirges
Raps that're really monologues
Rap editorials

Rap written on Post-it notes
Raps off the top of the dome
(because I don't write and I can make this handkerchief turn to a dove)

All types

I mean you got your gangster rap. Your underground rap. Your penthouse rap. Your satellite rap. Your nebula rap. Your heavenly rap.

Christian rap. Devil rap. Demonic rap. Angel rap. Emo rap. Nemo rap. Dory rap. Rap in its big boy pants. Rap in its Easter suit. Resurrection raps.

Black rap
Biracial rap
Polyracial rap
Political rap about these clowns

Clownish raps about the mimes
Oxymoronic rap
Rick Moranis rap
Shock rap
Horror-core
The rapping Coreys
Humpty rap

Poppy rap. Sesame seed rap. Grilled rap. BBQ rap. Cajun rap. Raps with
two horns. Raps with one horn aka uni-versal-rap. Rap for the blind. Rap
for the deaf aka Deaf Jams. Jelly rap. Nelly rap. Telly rap. Elmo rap. Big Bird
rap. Vegan rap. Raps made from Vegans.

And that's just rap
Don't get me started on hip-hop

# T.R.O.Y.

*If you're looking for lyrics,*
*if you're looking to cry,*
*if you're looking to think about life,*
*don't listen to hip-hop.*

—Post Malone

LL Cool J showed me how
to fold arms, plant sneakered feet
Pete Rock and CL Smooth showed me how
to reminisce a mosaic of moments
KRS-One, Public Enemy, X Clan
Big Daddy Kane and Queen Latifah helped me identify Africa
on a map, where Brooklyn, Compton & the Fifth Ward at
Black Thought, Lauryn Hill, Royce Da 5'9", Metal Face Doom
OutKast, A Tribe Called Quest, De La Soul, Del The Funkee Homosapien
made English a dance floor I could go on
on and on 'til break / dawn meet dusk

But maybe I'm just an old head, neck sore from looking back
Maybe the trap is a cloak and the pools produced by tear
tattoos too shallow to dive deep or maybe we've been here
before suffering the non-believers
auto-tuned filtered / every imperfection removed

# How to Rhyme in the Cipher

You won't be able to spot it
but you'll know when it's arrived

It takes at least three—answering each other's call
it don't take much time to accumulate
Three can become twelve can become thirty in seconds

You'll spot the most confident, they'll never let too much time pass
before driving spikes into air, God hands summoning power
punctuating each assonant empire

You'll spot the most experienced, listening, eyes like a falcon
waiting 'til moved to wash away all, with the poise of a giant

But as for you beginner
Get in early if you can, be inside the inner circle
close to the beatboxer

Perhaps there is trepidation
because of what the heads and toes carry
Or what's between your legs or stitched into your full name's lining
But the cipher is infinite enough to stretch
A zero, the cipher means nothing
No binary
No accumulation, no waste
No pieces, one unified wheel
No breaks just movement

So, when the ball is yours don't break
Share a solid eight the first time
premeditated, but incorporate something you see
the street name, the building backdrop, the time of day
Better yet, something someone else said, but be careful
don't spark a battle, don't talk about anyone's shoes
or facial acne or weight, make your eight specific, universal

Funny if you can, but if you're not funny
raunchy but if you're not raunchy
topical
Or just say whatever has to be born
And pass

Let the ball bounce around
when it comes your way again, give 'em eight more

Loosen up
(not too loose though)

If the most experienced is awakened from slumber
Never follow them, matter of fact,
the most experienced will usually close
But not always, sometimes the ball will keep bouncing
and you should stay there, until it is thrown over the fence
deflated or put to bed.

You're there to keep bouncing
to keep throwing energy into the center
staying close to the source
getting loose, huddled into a sacred cluster
where the heads concur
Saying yes, to the nothing
from something they've built

# Wu-Tang Is for the Children:
# An Ode to the Clean Version

Some remove the word, some reverse the word
*tihS* yeah!
Some supplement words with different words

We the car seat strapping, headphone carrying
salute you, you slightly deformed offering

To keep we who are 95% boom bap fed
We require a steady diet of dope in the measure

We who literally took one of those cornball
folksy CDs and chucked them out the window
*kcuF* that!

Only the real is heard between my four wheels
and every rapper who considers the buying power
of we rap parents should automatically win Grammys
and those who keep seven dirty words
off the menu entirely, get Nobels

Oh, edited PG-13 rated rap music!
Though you cease to be what you are without your glorious
gleaming gully grimy profane I appreciate your willingness to invert and
dismember yourself

And every rapper who considers how essential
pouring a foundation of low end for our children to walk upon is the true
GOAT

For the sake of tomorrow, the Ol' Dirty *dratsaB* said it best
and you don't argue with The Wu-Tang
they ain't nuthin to *kcuF* with

# DJ Khaled Loves You

You started out humble
You was a speck of light
Scattered shards of matter that decided
"We gon collaborate"
Like Method Man and Mary J

You Epic
An ocean you a Bellingham tulip field
You, a view from a first-class seat
The first fizzy sip out the
cold can of La Croix
Ironic because you hot

And they don't want you to be the comet you is
They got comments for days
Trolls in a haze

Fuck 'em

They don't want you to burn
They want you to simmer
On an old-timey stove
some wood-burning kerosene type shit
But you a whirlpool
State of the art, stainless steel
The kinda appliance LeBron got in his kitchen

You ready to shine
twelve rounds
No standing eight-count
No do-overs
One take—nailed it

Once in a lifetime
And somehow you was made to live forever

Like some kinda Egyptian mummy spirit
No appropriation

You the yin and the yang
No racial
The alpha and omega
No religious

You a complete set
No random pieces missing
Mint Condition
Matter fact Ima get that R&B group of the same name to sing you
Pretty Brown Eyes, you butterscotch and soaked vanilla beans in milk
You silk
Matter fact you better than silk
You ain't even been named
You the uncertain
And that's why I rock with you

Uncertainty but certainly
Lovely as checked mic
Warm headphones

That's why I got love
And my love for you
Is iconic, solid, the best

# Pop Off

After some racist rapper with a confederate flag
started kicking those time-tested hits
"Welfare Queen"
"Chicago is a war zone"
"Get off your knees Kaepernick"
and course "Muslims"

I let off some shots along the back of the bluebird
And an old friend shot back

It's not that rappers can't be conservative
hip-hop knows no political affiliation
hip-hop is also vulnerable to schisms and isms
done its share of damage, rocked
salt into bleeding wounds

It's an ocean which is to suggest
it'll soothe, wave, reflect light
but also tsunami, and play host
to all manner of hammerhead

A mountain, majestic from a distance
Up close all climb, gravel, brush playing host
to unknown poison fang

But undeniably concrete
built on the shoulders of protest movements
and street gangs, disenfranchised poor
who descended from disenfranchised poor

This old friend
who hugged my southern grandmothers
rationalizing for the blue cross that left
so many of my people discarded
that feeling—that verse I've yet to birth
280 characters will not contain

# Break Down

*After Kurtis Blow*

*In 1980,*
*when I was a 19-year-old*
*undergraduate in college,*
*some friends suggested we attend a party dressed*
*like rappers we listened to at the time,*
*like Kurtis Blow...*
*We dressed up*
*and put on wigs*
*and brown makeup.*

—Virginia Attorney General Mark Herring, February 2019

Black for the ink
Black like space
Black when you blink
And forget your race

You feel Black with drum
Black with the bass
So, put some Black right on your face

You put Black
on
your face
Black it up, Black it up, Black it up

Rap make you wanna be another man
You Black your face, Black your face

It's not racist, you're such a fan
You Black your face, Black your face

Serena, Obama, Uzi Vert
You Black your face, Black your face

It's just good fun don't mean to hurt
You Black your face, Black your face

Halloween party
Wig with dreads
You Black your face, Black your face

A klansman roped to someone dead
You Black your face, Black your face
You put Black
on your face
Black it up
Black it up
Black it up

Break down

Brown is the color
Of our skin
Endless shades resembling
Natural beauty & edible delights
But we ain't for consumption
Don't melt between molars
Tongue not easy swallowed
Speech not easy to digest

But the skin. . .

Black for the ink
Black like space
Black when you blink
And forget your race

You feel Black with drum
Black with the bass
So, put some Black right on your face

You put Black
on
your face
Black it up, Black it up, Black it up

And don't do it
don't do it, don't
do it, do it, do it!

Don't do it, don't do it, don't
do it, do it, do it!

Don't do it, don't do it, don't
do it, do it, do it!

# Harriet Tubman to Kanye West

*When you hear*
*about slavery for*
*four hundred years—for*
*four hundred years? That sound*
*like a choice!*

—Kanye West, Tuesday, May 2, 2018

My lights flash when my eyes squeeze
My head spin I been nodding since
that head-banger-blow to my dome
Since then the sky known my name

I had bars too
Linked iron
Hard knocks
Wild vivid colors
when things went Black

Misunderstood
I too operated along edges
splintered dead by winter

Some Black folk thought I was crazy too
My exploits, brought fear
but I died

Pistol grip
for the people

I too
*why'd* and *how come'd* and *maybe'd*
I too had the audacity of free thought
The audacity to fantasize
dark and holy
fantasies outside the twisted white line

They called me Moses, original rebel renegade
Must stay teeth, must stay

Fighting the century
To widen the breadth of choice

You got all the eras
at your fingertips
You can push the culture at the press of play
can blend what exist to transcendence
like we took the worst parts and built portals

If we hadn't stepped up
We'd still be inside
The intestines

Blind and burning as we suffocate
inside the bowels
but we crawled up from
The Crock-pot's bottom

We did this for you

We risked removal
we endured
were chopped and screwed
distorted like a sample

Didn't have time to slow jam
or press bodies close

During your accident
we whispered a message through the wire
*Save this one. He has work ahead.*
You were spared instrument
bruised to never forget
always rewind
listen to the voices on the track
before saying a word

# The Rain

*In Virginia there is a petition to replace a statue of
Christopher Columbus with a statue of Missy Elliot.*

—*The Huffington Post*, August 21, 2017

Hee Hee How
Hee Hee

How you even let it go this long
extended version / mix good
but mastering wrong

It's tragic, which is why I laugh
Hee Hee How you let it get this bad

Appreciate the ask
but statues can't dance
and you know how I like to
shake my future and past

The great fake late explorer
limb chopper, kiss my ass

I

Appreciate the honor
know the feelings imperative
rebel flag still flappin'
belt buckles still snappin'

Statues drop out like baselines
come down but hate
they can't bury it

Until they do
this Black woman rap
like the headdress on Harriet

Tubman

My body stay bumpin'
statues can't go clubbin'

So instead put a speaker
where that imposter stands

Bump my jams across colonial land
let the reverb disturb the buried
the disease they carried
plus, the echo who follow

Let my bounce caress the bruises
Every wound nurse it
whips, handcuffs

Put that thing down
flip it, reverse it

I live to
make you
feel alive

That's all I'm down for
don't prop me outside
I can't stand the downpour

# More Statues Need High Heels

*A community organizer in St. Paul, Minnesota, is petitioning the local govern-
ment to replace a statue of Christopher Columbus with a monument celebrating
Prince, September 2017.*

Dearly beloved,

You're gathered under my purple gaze against this twin city gray
You birthed this monument, copied and pasted me over another

Explorer, I too searched for new land, stood stern, firmly
Scanning a new plateau, I got lost too but I looked to the moon

It always led me to you and when I got to you I did not terrorize
I played you a tune, and now let us resume, bodies weren't built to last

But in this form, I can remind you daily

A blank face may say it all, and two cheeks say even more
Do not smile when a smirk is necessary

If you must, when you must throw shade
over the blinding glow of mediocrity, throw it hard

Know all the colors in a prism, feel the fabrics on the loom
Live between Funk and Rock, Batman and Joker

Between masculine, feminine, let the world know you're being enslaved
when your output is held captive, running its strings across bars

But do become slave to exploration, get lost, feel the waves
below the hull guide until you hit land

Climb down, let your Andre #1 heels collide with sand
of this land only new to you, listen for the metronome

And when invited release
all the past inside
all your Bootsy and Jimi and James

will kick sand to wind
your fingerprint etched onto every grain
will be carried across the Great Lakes
along interstates, farms, mountains
swamps and sewers
Curbs, corners, out car windows
up the side of the highest rises
through the antennas and out
across the galaxy

Bodies weren't meant to last
but the reverb dance eternal

But I have gone astray
forgive me I am dreaming

As I say this dreaming as explorers do
Through all space, through all time

# Give the People What They Want:
# A Second Ode to Isiah Thomas

According to Isiah Thomas a perfectly arched jump
shot that glides straight through the rim's middle
barely grazing the net is the true measure

He demonstrates this for all of us
adolescent dopes, disbelief, we are feet
away from the same guy who drew our screams
as he fought through the 1988 championship
coming millimeters short at the magical forum

Our hero, yet all we want to know
*why don't you dunk?*

His response is that beautiful
technically sound jump shot
from the three-point line

If our eyes weren't on it we wouldn't have heard it
He punctuates his statement with a satisfied scrunch of his face

And still we are unsatisfied
*How come you don't dunk?* turns into
*Can you even dunk?*

*Hmmm maybe he can't*
*The average player is 6' 7", Isiah is only 6' 1"*
*But Spud Webb is only 5' 7" and he's like the best dunker*
*Hey Isiah, is Spud Webb coming to the camp?*
*Hey y'all, stop asking him about dunks, he clearly can't dunk so let's just move on*

Cornered, Isiah sighs
opens his palms
His aid fills them with the ball

He scans our sugar-filled faces
Humbles himself
And gives us what our parents paid for.

# The Meaning of the Dunk

*Unbelievable creativity type of player.*
—Michael Jordan on Dominique Wilkins

We didn't invent it but we evolved it
Like the woodwind
The turntable
The grind
The dance floor

The blacktop lab
For physics, bioscience
For thermodynamics
linguistic alchemy

The Dunk the flashback
To the playgrounds
Where bodies become heroic
Leaping across the canyon

They can't stop
they can only hope to contain

The Dunk a fissure in time
A flashbulb
A call to celebrate
A Juneteenth jubilee contained

elegance airlessness
The crowd holding its breath
In anticipation
before
The tympany
Boom

The outlawed boom
The percussion live in the balls of feet
The squeak of the sneaker prelude
Before lift off
And here come that boom
Televised
In real time
Can't take it back
Can't apologize
In your face

We taught this whole world to boom
To send reverbs / echoes through space

The dunk science fiction
The dunk disruption
Volcano in the ebb and flow
Of regularly scheduled function

It's the solo

Praise Bill Russell    Louis Armstrong
Wilt Chamberlain    Mingus
Dr. J   Dizzy
Dominique   Miles Davis

Notes floating free though space
Your eyes on the body
made the slow mo
his canvas

Dark
In red

From the baseline

Michael Jordan—Coltrane
Spud Webb—Art Blakey

Rim shot
Darryl Dawkins—Cannonball
Shaquille O'Neal—George Clinton
the falling plexiglass
Showering over the heads
Baptizing the court
Christening the court
Under the jumbo screen's watchful eye

Praise all the artist of air
The Dunk
freestyle cipher
Display of airlessness
Limitless
crafty Br'er Rabbit snatch, grab
A riddle
¡Hallelujah!

Declaration
I am a man
Not a boy
I am alive
And defiant
A hero
I make deals with gravity
I rise and fall
The rim
The backboard
The game ain't over
But my name reverb
The Dunk is my signature

# Of the Lord

*For Dominique Wilkins*


Dominique mean "of the Lord"
Latin rooted, French
Black like Haiti

We like our names with
Peaks, slopes, and vowels

We like our names to be aerial
and aural, throat and teeth and tongue
Our names gotta be songs

Serena
Beyoncé
Kobe
Kareem
LeBron
Abdul
Kyrie
Toussaint
Andre
Kanye
Rashaan

Names that melt résumés
Draymond
DeAndre
Desiree

Shanice
Latice
Lashawna
Latoya
Kimani

Names that disrupt the roll call

Marshawn
Aaliyah
Malik
Layla

Idris

Like the names in holy books

Names that point to the world's faiths
coalesced here on this stolen continent

the european
the middle east

The whole lexicon
The field, court, globe
Palmed but never dominated

Give us
Onomatopoeia names
Names with naps
Names that's laid
That give shade
Names that glide
Like Clyde
That fly like MJ
Or feet sliding in white socks on *Motown 25*
Names with wings of predator birds
Names like Dominique

# Ashy to Classy: An Ode to Lotion

The TSA agent opens the teeth on the black travel bag
Likely the forgotten razor blades again
Instead the bottle of unscented shea butter the culprit

*Sorry sir, you have one too many lotions*

There are eight cardinal rules to safely navigate the world
One is don't give TSA agents a hard time
So I comply, and bid farewell to the new addition
of my moisturizing arsenal

Thankfully the eucalyptus aftershave lotion remained
And the accumulated hotel acquisitions
And of course my emergency coco butter bar

There are never too many lotions
One in my car, one in my wife's car

One never knows
After each handwashing before
the cracks begin to sting fingertips

Or crisp Minneapolis walks make lips look donut-glazed
Or arid New Mexico afternoons make space between
thumb and finger headstone gray

Can't be out here with elbows lookin' like a desert
Ankles lookin' parched
Kneecaps lookin' like they could sand tables smooth

Rough as it is out here, the relief
of skin's resurrection is a baptism

The body's largest organ makes joyful noise
With every glide of butter or oil
"Too many" you say

Nah! Never too much, never too much
Gotta be smooth as Vandross voice
Can't be out here lookin' like we been hugging ghosts

# Factory

*Liccy Dahl told BBC Radio 4 that when her late husband originally dreamed up Charlie and the Chocolate Factory, he imagined it starring "a little Black boy." It was his agent who thought it was a bad idea, when the book was first published, to have a Black hero. She said people would ask: "Why?"*

My little Black brown boy
devours Dahl with endless appetite
jokes about Trunchbull and the rest
critiques the film and stage adaptations
always wants to know why so much singing

His mother gave him all the words
His eyes learned to shape the letters while she read

I taught him to shape those letters
to stories across panels

For the long road ahead, we fuel
building him a factory, pillared by story, words strung
like lights so sweet he can almost taste them

Why? Why the hell not!?
We too crave new worlds that're not just
cautionary or oppressor's education
We too have known hunger
We too prayed the monsters be friendly

# Tao of House Party

*(Because sometimes pops is trippin')*


When them 'roided up bullies got you lifted
in the lunchroom, coins you pass off as dollars
shattering against the heavily bleached concrete
all eyes await the first balled ashy knuckle
sandwich against your grill
You say it's worth it because they disrespected moms

But Kid, place her honor across the scale
from a swollen mouth
what weighs more?

After all, tonight is your homie's party
your front door bolted closed
punishment for getting your face shocked in the lunchroom

Next time, chill, let it slide,
they not invited anyway

If you find yourself on punishment
and you must slip past passed out pops,
Dolemite rapping to his snoring face
ease that door careful, turn slow
because door handles do snitch

On your way to your homie's
when the cops stop to flashlight your face
lift hands high, palms flat as your haircut
breathe easy Kid but if you must run,
do it like hounds in earshot

Maneuver across unfamiliar backyards
leap over their fence like you Ferris trying to beat
mom to the garage and pray you land in a Black yuppie's

stiff backyard party, so you may show the DJ
how to put scratches over that smooth jazz
as God intended, but not too long Kid, a party awaits

And upon arrival, you'll see it was worth it
brothers and sisters, faded, crisp, gold chains
stretch pants, bright as a Vaseline-salved forehead

When your homie, the host, grabs the mic
and begins to rock, that is your moment

You must trade insults
and may they be sharp
as a barber's blade, slick
as a torso in groove

But your challenges won't appear solely on the mic
the dance floor will call, and there too you must
paint the room with those limbs, vanquish
anyone who step with a kick. Your opponents will be formidable
earrings alone could knock you out, but to win here
is to elevate spectator to participant, to transform dance floor
to blacktop, as the DJ swings a jump rope across the entire room
so all heads get singed by the burning roof

# Ferris Bueller's Black Friend

Eric was not among the sportos, motorheads, geeks,
wastoids, dweebies, or dickheads
who thought Ferris a righteous dude

He knew Ferris before high school fame
back when he used to rock a yarmulke
to school and was asked repeatedly to reveal horns

Just like Eric was asked to show his tail and webbed feet
they hid from those same motorheads and sportos
who now cover Ferris's tracks, considering his victories theirs

They still cool
though since Sloane and Cameron
they don't see each other too much

But he was supposed to skip school with them
He tried to pull a fake fever but got an earful
from his father about how many paper routes
and trucks and how hard he worked to get them
in that neighborhood

His father takes no days off
Why give them an excuse to celebrate and plot
in your absence?

# The Walking Dead

Imagine them, unjustly murdered legions returned
their graves too loose to block out the world's debate

They don't want to eat cortexes and frontal lobes
A dangerous imagination got 'em out here staggering
blasting beams of light through their ventilated flesh
looking to close the loop on unfinished business

Selling enough CDs and other sundries
finishing this cigarette and going about my drive
to get grandson's school supplies home
all of the mundane chores that give life its shade

To get to work, to get to the chapel
to bow head in submission to high powers
but interrupted by a murder in flight

Since the only thing more restless than bones
are the worms dancing through them
They don't rest but wander, ambling on,
dragging limbs like baggage trying to close the loop

# Game of Thrones

*The creators of* Game of Thrones *are developing a series that takes place in an alternate timeline, where the Southern states have seceded from the Union, giving rise to a nation where slavery remains legal.*

As if the effects and echoes of said institution do not linger
As if we can't still taste the flakes of horror in the wind
As if the rebel flag is not still brazenly snapping air and buckling belts

As if this series hasn't already played out in the mind
of every racist since 1865
As if this premise hasn't already played out in the mind
of every Black person since the first hulls of prison buses filled

As if the tangled vines of this jungle do not choke the life
in full view, captured in smartphones across the ocean

So much tragedy on this real timeline
So many unheralded
So many buried
So many hidden
crippled gagged

So many bad guys fly off on private jet wings
Smash through oil clouds like blood-red pitchers of Kool-Aid,
So many bad kings passed out in gold thrones
cradling war spoils from battles they ain't even fight

The story of even fictional land
still penned by the winners
Even if they attended progressive schools
Even if their hearts bleed on screen

They can mold any bodies they want
Project them through their lens
and the box office they call home keeps they cash pillows fluffed

Meanwhile

We feel the ancestors at our shins
Hear them gasp, shriek, beg and pray
for our further existence, we are beyond even their imagination

We are the alternate
Makers on the margins
now alive daily renaming

Rebirthed, remixing
Stepping defiantly over legacy's bones
Daily heating the sands
to see ourselves reflected
The margin
made central
essential

Our visions
assembled
with so much precision
It could be reality

# Taken

The takers talkin' 'bout some *take the country back*

Because all they know is take

Took away lands from the indigenous
Took the Indian and "saved the child"
Took the profile, the headdress, the names, the profit

Took Africans

Took the Bible, made it a noose
Took the cross, set it blazing

Took Japanese
Took Semitic lives
Took limbs of poplars
Adorned them with bleeding ornaments

Took pictures

Took time to hear the case
Heard the case
Took it to the furnace
Hid ashes under the bed
Took the sheets off and cut eye holes

Take and take
Take this
Take that
Take that

Took
Jazz
Blues
Dance

Moves
Dap
Dab
And made 'em cornball
Wack-ass Pat Boone Elvis Vanilla Ice
Justin
Timber-take

Took publishing
Took credit
Took up all the space
All four walls of the library
All the gunpowder in the cannon

And when we took
samples for our raps
you took us to court

When it's you who took
them cookies out the cookie jar

*Take that*
*Take that*
*Take that*

Take our leaders to the grave
Take their visages
dismember
distort
appropriate their message

Use their message to sell this
Sell that

Need to
Take a seat
Take a step back

But you cannot take it
In the dark

So, you cry about taking
When all you do is take

Take this
Take that

But we won't be took
Hoodwinked
Or bamboozled

We can't be taken to the river
and told not to drink
We hungry, never thirsty
Ice Cube over the phone
*special sets of skills homie*

All of us
won't be
Cannot be
Never ever
again
Taken

# How to Listen to Gospel:
# An Ode to Naomi Shelton

I remember when mom took the needle off
—Anita Baker, Terence Trent D'Arby—
We couldn't hear The Whispers begin to rock
or Quincy Jones Jazz fuse Moe Dee and Dizzy

For a while around our suburban home
it was all the good news, Sounds of Blackness
Kirk Franklin, big choirs multiplied Nell Carter
with robes swaying like shoulders in time

Every Sunday at New Calvary Baptist
it was all she needed but I needed more
I was eighteen one foot out

Toward Chicago where I could turn the volume up on
strictly hard-core reality where God

was expressed in the cipher, a sovereign utopia where I would blackout
catch the ghost and string tongues
like dried peppers on a New Mexico porch

Making claims and setting fire to paths and bridges behind
Like the young are prone to do

These days on the other side of forty
my cipher rings of deadlines, google calendars, requests, doors
and no, disappointments, have to, sometimes the volume goes mute

And when silence tightens, here you come

You been singing since high school
but didn't record until you were in your sixties

You are seasoned
paprika in that voice. All that Alabama,
all that disappointment, all that release
The way you give it away. You alchemize it to light
and send it back down the tracks of history

Your face on the cover reminds me of my mom's mom
who always had peppermints to cool us out
with one hand formed pound cakes
the other, directed us to sapling trees
with adequate arms for swatting the wicked from us

# The *Wiz* Live from the Brown Theatre, Louisville, KY, December 2018

When *The Wiz* came to Louisville Black folk showed up
We donned our best to sing along to the songs
for songs we deem ours will forever be sacred

When *The Wiz* came to Louisville we remembered the time
we first saw Michael crucified in makeup and straw
his voice indistinguishable and possibly higher than Diana's
Nipsey Russell all silver and in his feelings

We remembered our uncles and aunties and cousins
belting and humming *Ease on Down*

So, when we heard *The Wiz* was coming to Louisville we paid
and it wasn't cheap, but this is sacred and at the classy Brown theatre no less
and it stars Shirley Murdock, as the tradition of Black shows dictate

The play must star an R&B singer of eras past
like self-respecting children of Motown
we shelled out the dough and we paid for the parking

Sat down, and of course they played Erykah Badu's live album, as we waited
while a brother made his way down the aisles selling programs
for five dollars we realized what this was going to be

Not *The Wiz* of our childhood, with Billboard's best and brightest
this would be the kind that sold programs for five dollars
The curtain will go up twenty minutes late
revealing a stage naked save for a confused actor and
an empty projection surface, and in that moment, you know
no tornado coming to sweep us away

No tornado came to sweep us away that Sunday at 3 p.m.
Just a collective groan, a wave across our chest
that time, like Michael's mind, gone

We forgot that at the end of the film Richard Pryor steps
out behind the wall
face bloated from the reckless '70s
no giant but a mere man with imagination

In the end *The Wiz* was a con
(not that we stayed 'til the end)
As swiftly as we bought tickets we retreated
eager as Dorothy's ruby heels

# Lil Nas X Brings the Country Together

The drum is a planet vast enough
to hold anything so everything
is liable to end up in the stew
And when I saw them West End
middle schoolers rock to it
I knew some forgot who built
billboards in the first place

Must've forgot the origin of
drum, banjo, and bass
Forgot about how we landed, the field
and corrals and hollars

Holler, the music was segregated
Like the people for a reason
Rock 'n' roll just Black slang for
Sex, coined because R&B was just
sped up blues and blues was how
people healed

The blues a universal
American noise like country
One of the genres people leave out when they say
*I listen to everything but. . .*

Genre is a satellite inside a pocket

Hip-hop opens its velvet rope
to all as long as it can fit
over the drum where anyone

is liable to end up looking
back at you smiling the same smile

so much can be carved thin enough
To fit in a pocket / sold and spread across
corners of a nation but everything belongs to the beat

# An Invitation from a Tribe Called Tomorrow to Those Broken by Today (2019 Remix)

Our roots are scattered fields
convergence of shades
Shapes over the cyclical
myths merged with music
Double-dutching time

Fighting equality across passing seconds
Collapsed and coalesced into a Sam Cooke melody

The static jumping off beat machines
We sing bridges to reconnect our outcasts and outliers
To solidify the roux

We are a tribe made up of other tribes who've wandered
Born of states and states of mind
professions, majors and minors
All who wandered away

A tribe of deserters who heard the calls
pushed through vines and brush
sliced thickets of confusion
found one another

We hear the calls, the waves
The only thing that can live in space
Static-y signals that reverberate to our members who've seen brighter stars
But we don't need no mothership to crush, literally into the room
like the hand of Zeus and scoop us to a nest

This is an invitation

We believe in the non-hierarchical nature of how things grow
We believe that leadership depends on the size of the path, of the hill
We believe in the renewable energy of invention
It's how we fight—we make weapons of our laughter
We believe in the sanctity of joy

The word for work is service
The word for play is holiness
We do not know the word supremacy
Unless speaking of Coltrane's love

Apology is our word for justice
We believe in reparation, repair, reconciliation
these are the words for evolution

We believe in color, so of course we see it
Appreciate the melanin or lack of
Recognize the stories they tell, the fears it dies to overcome

Brown skin
Beige skin
Clear skin
Wrinkled skin
Smooth freckled skin
Dark
Bright
Rough
Scarred skin
All shall be anointed
with that coconut oil

We recognize the inherent fluidity of identity and flesh
Bellowing pronouns across rooms
Moving like waves of water throughout the air
Throughout the air and highways we send calls

48

Like this one

And if it ripples through you
then you are invited

You are invited to walk with us
Dance or sit, watch how we release
And refilter the deathly echoes of the world
chimneys of polluting rhetoric
Chemicals making every sea a dead one
The abusive projectiles of the world

We are a tribe but belong to the world

This is an invitation to you

Who've been bruised by the rising
of what has always scarred this nation of tribes
Dominated by a few, who manifested themselves

Bearing their crest of the wild dog
Whose earthbound custodians of afterlife
promises can be bought or reassigned with impunity

To you who've been disillusioned
Disappointed, diluted

This invitation to channel
the furious, fervent, urgent pushing
The world in your immediate radius
To exalt the stars who float among you
The dimmed and dented among you
To recognize the volcanic possibility waiting to be invited
To move
*We do not rest*
*We believe in vigilance*
*We wear the crest*

*of patience*
*The crest of the tortoise and the fox*
*Open the locks*
*Fluid our borders*
*Tellers of stories*
*True life reporters*
*Magical minds*
*Ignoring the orders*
*And rules to protect*
*The dominant sect*
*Earthly intents*
*Making the most of mourns and laments*
*Tribe of the watchers*
*Current events*
*The Fergusons Standing Rocks and the Flints*
*Sparked by those in positions who bend*
*Break the brutal rules made by men*
*Not here to offend*
*But let's not pretend*
*Yes, we've made sins*
*But ask, "do we make profit off them?"*

*You are invited*

*Come be delighted and ignited to spin*
*Rotate like the world and the mixes and blends*
*Tribe of the DJ, Tribe of heat wave*
*Cradling fire to light up each day*

*And we a tribe called tomorrow*
*Filling the hollow*
*Speaking to reunite with each breath and swallow*
*Coast to coast*
*The ghost they follow*
*And they remind us*
*To stand up to sorrow*
*Protect one another*
*Every hair every bone to the marrow*
*Uncover the fallacies of the pharaohs*

*Tribe of tomorrow / futuristic we seem*
*But our word for tomorrow is dream*
*Our word for tomorrow is dream*

# Lost in Space, August 23, 2016

Grocery store, the usual, trying to get in, get out
List—produce, pastas, grains crossed out—here we go
Almost done, one item to go, deli counter

An elderly woman, spunky, late seventies, Caucasian pushes back
With a devious smile, playful granny
I play along
*I'm almost outta here anyway*
In our fooling around, the box of sparkling water falls

She apologizes
"No problem" I lie
thinking of the explosions when I open the can

She has taken this as invitation

She reaches into the cart
"What are these anyway?"
Grabbing the bottle of my favorite iced tea

She fixes her face, indignant
"You people have to have everything"

My mind scrolls through the "what she could've meant?" files
Maybe she means young people
"You young people have to have everything"
I reply "You have no idea"

I go into robo-banter, passive-aggressive patter crafted careful
Over thirty plus years as the diversity-in-the-room, the few of a few
navigating, clutching my identity, pressing my self-respect
to force the water out my lungs

I don't even know what I'm saying
Or why I'm continuing to engage

"Well, I have more money than you" she says

I launch back, "Like I said, you have no idea"
Somehow, I manage to disengage, soon
as I turn away I notice the younger woman
around my age, Caucasian, who watched
the whole thing

Thinking, surely, she will meet my eyes with a shake of the head
Instead she offers "Oh she did the same thing to me"

A pacification of the lava. A "You think you got it bad. . ."
A plea for me not to write this to reflect this to take it to heart
For me to not call it what it is

The ability to claim space, hold space, feel safe in it. That is freedom.
The ability to invade space with minimal to absolutely no consequence is
power

As I walk to the parking lot, to unload
a car rolls by, playing news radio, dispatches from a nation in a gutter

Suddenly the world's narrative feels like it can fit
in my trunk next to the spoils
The pastas, grains, produce, and the shaken cans
I hope will settle by the time I get home

# Avengers

A mild-mannered Newark airport
and from the groggy eye's corner
A family rocking yarmulkes
That look like Captain America's shield

An image ricochets, the first issue,
Where Captain is punching the führer square
in the mustache while bullets bounce off the shield

Born from apostle minds Simon and Kirby in '41
This super augmented goy stitched
In the country's blood dream and pride
A bright, action-packed flash of possibility

Can we be Davids of Goliath's size?
Can faith alone protect our flesh?
Or will wit be our weapon finest honed?

All of the smiles and quips ricochet
Across this gate of weary travelers
We feel safer with them, as we line up to board

My uncovered mind wandering
plots of how to armor my own

# Breaking Sweat

PART ONE:

"Cardio"

I have joined a gym

Exercise an occasional fling
a once in a while *oh you again*
But the life expectancy of a Black man is sixty-seven

On that treadmill
I walk, not too fast
Just trying to warm up

The televisions lined above peer down smirking
As I increase speed—cautiously
Taking it easy
Not trying to be no hero

Above
Today's latest cell phone video is dissected

Opposing neckties
Side by side
vertical rectangles
Ping-pong their way through the familiar

Closed-caption tries to keep up

I am walking a little faster now

A new headline visual
The desert blows a thin beam of smoke
back up toward the sky that struck it

before commercials for insurance
and faster internet

Around me machines whir
and bodies grunt and grasp for air

A symphony pushing its presence
through the hip-hop in my headphones

When we return
The CDC says certain threats are inevitable
Certain viruses have our names and addresses

So do these drones
we are told we're destined to meet

Now I'm jogging
Slowly (you know)

Inside my headphones
Kendrick Lamar declares our survival

But I ain't here to be alright
thirty dollars will not be directly withdrawn from my checking account
on a monthly basis for alright

Nah we gon be better than alright
All of us
Under these fluorescent lights

The other new parents out to acquire the hourglass
The wounded warriors learning new limbs

The seniors, here to shake the alright colors
from our straining tendons

We look down to watch numbers
slowly make their climb

Calories
Heart Rate
Elapsed time

We add up death tolls along borders—In deserts
But also—classrooms—
and even city streets on a Sunday morning

And we in this workshop
This body shop
This sweat house of best intention
This church of kinetic holiness
We thank God for that safety

As we sweat

Each of us

running for our lives

PART TWO:

"Another Black Body"

This body is mine
But, also, political
When it stands, how it walks
with a bop
that's centrifugal

This body was once considered 3/5 of a human's

This body birthed by a woman
Who was birthed by a woman in a city of black alloy
This body fled before the rust settled
This body nomadic
Moving through zip codes propelled by static

This body don't do neckties
it wears hoodies
ball caps
T-shirts
sneakers
This body needs freedom

This body stay in headlines

Hunted
Some say
Hated
Some say

This body celebrated when adorned with gold and vest
And nine shot ventilated by smith and wes

This body know hunger
This body starved
Yes
This body get stress

This body knows love
shows love
never held guns
never sold drugs

This body is Black
Since birth
African
American

This body got DNA of a slave master
This body got a Master's Degree
And still this body ignorant
Sometimes, foolish, full of it

This body push iron
And keeps trying
This body a gazelle
This body is a lion
This body is a prayer
To never know cell
got blood
got heart
This body keep moving
This body's a shark
This body's an ocean

This body swings
Grooves, Moves, Rhythm
sliiiiiiiiiiiiiiiiiides electric

This body don't know how to Dougie!

This body get ugly
Don't pop bottles
Not bubbly
This body pop and lock
They trying to lock this body to a gurney
This body needs attorneys

It's known rivers
searching for the mountaintop
This body trying to know itself

This body survives
endures
makes mistakes
wasn't no mistake

This body got two hands
That clap
Salute
Give dap
Two hands Black-hand sided
Become fists
Legs that sprint
When the rope get ignited

Political
The subject in headline
a force that's centrifugal
Behind the hashtag
This body is mine
To protect
To cherish
Mine
to deprive
This body is fed
well
This body is alive

# Bonus Track: Say My Name

I always thought it just came out of a book

My mother still has it
looks homemade, the cover
crude and orange

*African Names*

Inside the book it says something like *Idris means everlasting* or *never to die*
but I don't think that's right

My mother Pat, my dad Don, their parents Thelma, James, Ruth and also
James

Their siblings
Alicia, Ron, Theresa, Darrin, Reginald, Janet, Joyce, Jay, Val, Alvin, James
Jr.—they wanted to break the chain

They were Afro-wearing 1960s Black power children
trying to make a statement through their offspring
wanted us to have names with throat and vowels

In Detroit, they were a minority, our Black church asked,

*Why you give that boy that African name? that Muslim name?*

*There are names in the Good Book—strong Apostle names*

*Names in the phone book—strong regular names*

In the suburbs, I was a minority, my white middle American school asked,
*Is it eye-dris?*
*IDI-ris?*
*I'd rice?*
*Isadore?*

*Ivan?*
*Iggy?*
*Can I just call you I?*
*Can I call you E?*
*Can I call you something*
*other than your name?*

Age 11, I ask my mom, can I change my name to something else? *Tony, Mark, Sean—something else?*

Being named Idris in North America will arrest people

You must grow patience

*What an interesting name*
*That's so unusual*

*Sounds Turkish*
*Sounds Greek*
*Are you Muslim?*

*Where does it come from?*

Age 16, two Arab guys come through my register
get big-eyed when they see my name tag

They're curious
how the name found its way to a Target in suburban Michigan

They're disappointed when I tell them about *African Names*

Age 28, I am in the Middle East, where they pronounce it beautifully not all straightened and flattened
*E-Dreece*

They have given it a joyful bounce

*Idris is a prophet*
*in the Quran*

Earlier—Age 20, new to Chicago, broke, cleaning cigarette butts  out of
the restaurant urinal for minimum wage, my boss, a giant stereotype with
turtleneck, sport coat, big glasses, and thick-as-Ditka's-mustache accent—
unzips at the urinal

(Yep, the one I just cleaned)

He smirks *I ain't gonna remember that name of yours. How 'bout I just call you*
*Eddie*

And my name became Eddie until his assistant suggested that he stop for
fear I would claim cultural insensitivity

The gentleman from the UK tells me the Welsh have a myth

*There is Morocco's Moulay Idris*

*The jazz world's Idris Muhammad*

*There is the other theater artist Idris Ackamoor*

*Television's Idris Elba*

*What does it mean?*

*Fiery poet—prophetic cashier—confused minority*

*What does it mean?*
*Confused minority*
*Black power baby—*

*It's so exotic*
*What is it again?*

*Philosophic cleaner of urinals*

*I ain't gonna remember that*
*That's gonna take me a while to learn*

*Old, young, Black, white, the spectrum*

*What does it mean?*
*How do you say it?*

*I call myself E-Dreece*
*like my mama says it*
but who knows if she's saying it right

# ABOUT THE AUTHOR

**IDRIS GOODWIN** is a creative voice for change impassioned by the power of art for social good. An award-winning playwright, producer, educator, father, and occasional rapper, Goodwin coined the term "breakbeat poet." He is the author of the Pushcart–nominated essay and poetry collection *These Are the Breaks*. His publications with Haymarket Books include the award-winning *Inauguration,* cowritten with Nico Wilkinson, *Human Highlight: Ode to Dominique Wilkins*, and the controversial play *This Is Modern Art*, both cowritten with Kevin Coval. His words, voice, and sometimes entire body, have shown up on HBO Def Poetry, Sesame Street, NPR, BBC Radio, and the Discovery Channel. He has received support from the NEA and the Ford, Mellon, and Edgerton Foundations, as well as the Playwrights' Center's McKnight Fellowship. His widely produced stage plays include *And in This Corner: Cassius Clay, How We Got On*, and *Hype Man: A Breakbeat Play*. A frequent public speaker at conferences and educational spaces, Idris is one of the leading voices in his field, and he is committed to using art to cultivate more diverse and equitable spaces. Idris and his family live in Louisville, Kentucky, where he is the producing artistic director of Stage One, a professional theater company for young audiences. For upcoming performances, content, and creative writing tools visit www.idrisgoodwin.com.

# ABOUT HAYMARKET BOOKS

Haymarket Books is a radical, independent, nonprofit book publisher based in Chicago. Our mission is to publish books that contribute to struggles for social and economic justice. We strive to make our books a vibrant and organic part of social movements and the education and development of a critical, engaged, international left.

We take inspiration and courage from our namesakes, the Haymarket martyrs, who gave their lives fighting for a better world. Their 1886 struggle for the eight-hour day—which gave us May Day, the international workers' holiday—reminds workers around the world that ordinary people can organize and struggle for their own liberation. These struggles continue today across the globe—struggles against oppression, exploitation, poverty, and war.

Since our founding in 2001, Haymarket Books has published more than five hundred titles. Radically independent, we seek to drive a wedge into the risk-averse world of corporate book publishing. Our authors include Noam Chomsky, Arundhati Roy, Rebecca Solnit, Angela Y. Davis, Howard Zinn, Amy Goodman, Wallace Shawn, Mike Davis, Winona LaDuke, Ilan Pappé, Richard Wolff, Dave Zirin, Keeanga-Yamahtta Taylor, Nick Turse, Dahr Jamail, David Barsamian, Elizabeth Laird, Amira Hass, Mark Steel, Avi Lewis, Naomi Klein, and Neil Davidson. We are also the trade publishers of the acclaimed Historical Materialism Book Series and of Dispatch Books.